AF291250

Introduction

His new piece, the CD ROM *Encyclopædia*, tells you everything you need to know about Alan Currall. Deft in its approach, deceptive in its ambition, unfailingly droll and utterly disarming, it encapsulates all of the qualities that have distinguished this Glasgow-based artist's work over the last few years.

Encyclopædia is only one of a series of equally witty and inventive pieces to be covered in this publication, which incorporates a copy of the CD ROM and is released to coincide with the larger touring exhibition *Encyclopædia and other works*. First staged at Potteries Museum and Art Gallery, Stoke-on-Trent and Stills, Edinburgh during Spring/Summer 2000, this exhibition represents the first major survey of Currall's video and digital media work.

This publication, like the exhibition of the same name, is the result of a collaboration between a number of individuals and organisations. I would particularly like to single out Lucien Cooper at Potteries Museum and Art Gallery and Kate Tregaskis at Stills for their long-term commitment to the project, and Mark Dey at West Midlands Arts for his support of the publishing initiative.

Steven Bode
Director, Film and Video Umbrella

Down to Earth – Claire Doherty

Susan Sontag once wrote in an infamous diatribe on Diane Arbus that her photographs were the products of a "tourist in other people's reality".[1] In the present climate of unprecedented access to and appetite for 'real life', such criticism seems anachronistic. The dramatic impact of digital and on-line technology has transformed the production and reception of private footage in the public realm. Across a diverse range of media from contemporary photography to televisual docu-soaps, a co-dependent relationship between observer and everyday subject has become not only implied, but also explicit.

In Britain, popular entertainment in the late 1990s became synonymous with voyeurism by consent. The situation comedy, a one-time staple of television schedules, has been replaced by docu-soaps such as *Hotel, Airport, Children's Hospital* and *Paddington Green* (BBC). The paradox (and partly the attraction) of such programmes is that, whilst promoted as unscripted and spontaneous, the observed play to camera, becoming TV personalities in their own right. As one media commentator noted, "it adds a twist to the Warhol maxim about fame: in the future, everyone will be ordinary for 15 minutes".[2]

In response, comic parodies such as Chris Langham's *People Like Us* (BBC) and fictional scenarios such as Caroline Aherne's *The Royle Family* (BBC) and Alan Bennett's *Talking Heads* (BBC) have located the quotidian at the centre of small screen entertainment, gaining significantly high viewing figures. More recently, TV production companies, recognising a winning formula, have developed the fly-on-the-wall format *ad nauseum*, dropping 'people like us' into extreme contexts – a desert island in *Castaway 2000* (BBC) and a life without mod cons in *The 1900 House* (Channel 4).

Though the signature style of this genre is the overt complicity of the subject (with frequent asides to camera), its success lies in its close correlation to British comedy. The trademark amateur as hero, celebration of eccentricity and self-depreciating humour are all in evidence. At a time of acute crisis for English identity, these televisual 'realities' are mediated through a familiar, thoroughly English style, which corresponds to that of the Ealing films of the 1940s and 1950s. Historically this genre also relates to the English artist's "predisposition to depict mundane, everyday scenes, full of humorous incident" – the most obvious forebear being Hogarth.[3]

The flurry of critical analyses that accompanied the launch of Tate Britain and the British Art Show earlier this year were keen to associate the likes of Tracey Emin, Dean Hughes and Grayson Perry with this thoroughly British tendency to elevate the domestic to heroic status. Whilst the everyday seems to provide an infinite source of material for the writers of TV drama and comedy, so too the spectacular artistic gesture has been eclipsed by a self-conscious engagement with the experience of real life in contemporary art practice. Moreover, the preponderance of humorous oddballs and visual puns locates this work within the lineage of British comedy.

Thus, what links the diverse artistic practices of Alan Currall, Gillian Wearing, Darren Almond, Adam Chodzko, Graham Fagen, Richard Billingham, Martin Parr and Nick Waplington is the possibility of the ordinary to speak universally through familiar and humorous devices. The work of these artists is characterised by a reassuringly informal, non-professional subject matter. It engages the viewer through a process of identification and subversion. It intrigues precisely because it appears to speak a common language,

1 Susan Sontag, "America, Seen Through Photographs, Darkly", *On Photography*, 1977
2 Michael Collins, *Truth to Tell, The Observer*, Sunday 6 February 2000
3 See Nikolaus Pevsner, *The Englishness of English Art*, Penguin Books, London, 1964 and Julian Stallabrass, "The Britishness of British art", *High Art Lite*, Verso, 1999, pp. 225-257

though what is being said may be unfamiliar, quirky, epic or unnerving. As a result, some of these works also operate according to a critical category termed the 'urban pastoral' by critics Julian Stallabrass and Thomas Crow – a term which could equally be applied to the coercive tactics of 'reality TV'.

Julian Stallabrass, in his analysis of British art in the 1990s entitled *High Art Lite*, questions whether the viewer's position in relation to the ordinary subject is one of condescension; and the process of representation, one of exploitation. In comparing Billingham's family portraits to the genre of the pastoral, for example, Stallabrass suggests, "they are indeed a picture, still and without the possibility of change, and there is a certain paradoxical comfort to be gained from their constancy, even if it is a constancy of degradation, of what is in legend a particularly British stoicism and resilience, in the face of the tempest of modernity."**4**

Whether one agrees with Stallabrass (there is, after all, a tendency to generalise in *High Art Lite* about the social demographics of new audiences for art), his problematising of the apparent accessibility of the ordinary subject is crucial to an investigation of this genre. The pastoral, he argues, has been transferred from the rural to the urban and operates to affirm the primacy of the viewer's status over the observed subject, whose ability to 'speak' is silenced and ability to act is suppressed. More specifically he updates Susan Sontag's critical analysis of documentary photography, applying it to a wider cultural sphere, to work that, to date, has been legitimated by the global art world as democratic.

Alan Currall's vignettes operate strategically within this field of representation, playing to the current British enthusiasm for 'reality TV' and, seen in relation to Stallabrass's analysis of the complexities of the production and reception of mediated 'real life', Currall's work emerges as a curious, open-ended proposition.

As an English-born artist resident in Scotland, Currall has shown work across the world, from Melbourne to New York, Berlin to Stoke-on-Trent. I refer to the circulation of his work globally (that is within the confines of the global art world) because viewing his series of home movies is akin to receiving 'letters from home'. Home is quite clearly the British Isles, while the informal, deadpan tone, the off-the-cuff delivery, low-tech format and sheer eccentricity of his video pieces (instructing a micro-chip circuit-board in *Word Processing*, describing his life as an alien among us in *Jetsam*) serve to heighten an overall sense of understated English-ness – as discussed above in relation to the televisual format. As a body of work, his videos and most recent epic *Encyclopædia* act as fragments of life on earth. As if communicating to the alien associates of his *Jetsam* character, Currall's works emerge as social experiments or observations, which eschew the spectacular in favour of an analysis of the everyday.

Using an economy of means, Currall's video pieces function out of a territory of boredom. His locations are unremarkable and largely unimportant. This lack of artifice extends from subject to format. His hand-operated camera techniques serve to indicate a lack of theatricality and to intensify a sense of the real. Their emphasis throughout is on what is being said, often appearing incongruous to the context in which it is uttered. On one level, the subject is irrelevant. After all, who cares how many different ways he can say,"you're fired", which word he first learnt to speak, what his parents think would happen in the event of a ship-wreck, an air crash or a nuclear war, or what kind of definitions people might give for the words death or body? Somehow Currall makes us want to know. He keeps us watching.

Currall's scenarios, though seemingly unstaged, are highly schematic – revealed in the successive use of repetition. In *Telephone Conversation*, *I Know You're There*, *Lying About Myself In Order to Appear More Interesting* and *Survival Kits*, our patience becomes tested by the sheer monotony of the dialogue, but our sensitivity to what is being said is heightened as a result. Whilst works such as the tripartite *Survival Kits* or *Jetsam* coax and flatter the viewer with familiar references, from hearthside family gathering to confessional monologue, a surprising shift occurs in the dialogue. In both cases the subject is extreme, unbelievable,

Claire Doherty

unrelated to the visual clues we are given. It is precisely this tension between familiarity and distance that operates in direct opposition to the genre of the 'real' in contemporary artistic practice and popular entertainment.

–

Currall lulls the viewer into a false sense of security. The hearthside scene of *Survival Kits*, for example, appears cosy and familiar and increasingly claustrophobic as a result. Wearing his 'Christmas jumper', back to the fireplace, framed by the torsos of his seated parents, Currall appears locked into an adult's experience of going home, blithely turning the subject of conversation onto something bizarre as a method of surviving the ritual family visit. The ticking of the clock and restlessness of the dog serve to heighten this sense of repression. It is only the perversity of the disaster scenarios that saves us from boredom. In contrast to the direct engagement of the monologues in *Encyclopædia*, here the talking heads are removed from the frame. The facial characteristics and eye contact of the trio are out of sight, transforming the scene into a diorama over which the dialogue is laid.

–

There are strains in *Survival Kits* of Raymond Briggs' *When the Wind Blows* (Jimmy Murakami, 1987) – an animated film in which an elderly couple prepare with provincial naivety for the onset of nuclear war. Currall's parents dispense homespun advice based upon Currall's set questions. "Where is the best place to be when the plane/ship goes down? How would I get home? What would I eat?" They seem oblivious to the futility of plasters and aspirin in the face of nuclear fall-out or hypothermia. Yet, as a social experiment, the exercise reveals a great deal about his parents. Their replies are gendered, culturally, politically and socially specific. Their answers bear the hallmarks of a post-war generation, peppered with vague logic gleaned from mainstream film. Currall as always remains elusive.

–

Rather than promoting 'simple wisdom' over the academic as a triumphal endorsement of democracy, Currall consciously employs the mechanisms of 'reality TV' and the 'urban pastoral' with his tongue firmly in his cheek. Yet, what prevents his work becoming essentially patronising is the subversion of format through technique and dialogue/monologue. The viewer is always made aware of the nature of construction. As a result, his works unravel, rather than affirm, preconceptions.

–

Currall's shifting presence in the work indicates the unreliability of his material. He plays to camera, addressing an unspecified viewer, challenging our preconceptions about what we think we are seeing. *Lying About Myself In Order to Appear More Interesting* is perhaps the most revealing in this respect. Narrating the provenance of various items such as a straw hat, a squirrel mug and picture book, Currall embellishes his life, echoing the protestations of Walter Mitty. Not only does the title indicate the falsity of his assertions, but visual clues such as the sales sticker on his 'first picture book' also conflict with the intimate details communicated to us. Equally the *trompe l'oeil* qualities of *Sit* or *Lap*, the surrealism of *Jetsam* and Heath Robinson science of *Word Processing* reward us with a knowing wink to the real. A laugh or snigger is an indication that the work is doing its job – affirming our perception of the real by questioning it.

–

Currall is not interested in the truth, because he understands the subjectivity of its mediation. He is, however, interested in truths, essentially how we see the world individually and together as culturally, socially and politically formed beings. As a result, he uses humour to reward and unnerve the viewer. It is his exploration of the mechanism by which English humour operates that allows the work to problematise affirmation.

–

Encyclopædia is Currall's most comprehensive analysis of human behaviour to date. Produced at a time in which the government's policy for museums and galleries is based upon a broad notion of social inclusion, this work appears initially to democratise the dissemination of knowledge. Definitions are proffered by decontexualised, unidentified people – all of whom it is revealed in the accompanying literature have a direct relation to Currall himself. Their identities are formed only through their use of language, the relation of the word in question to their own experience. Through the immediacy and tone of the vox pop format, this work relates to Currall's earlier video pieces, yet crucially the relationship of the viewer to subject is explicit here. Interaction enables the viewer to choose what they want to hear about and whether to keep listening. Through their choices the viewer articulates his/her own identity in relation to those mediated on screen.

Crucially these works play to the implied democratisation of television and contemporary art practice against a backdrop of disenfranchisement. As documents of life on earth (or more specifically life on a small island), they indicate the insecurity of employment, the collapse of religious faith, the dominance of American mass culture and most effectively our insignificance in relation to technological and political systems. Currall achieves a critical, social engagement, employing the devices of humour and characterisation which are used elsewhere in televisual docu-drama to affirm hierarchy and existing systems of belief.

In reference to the social limits of *High Art Lite*, Julian Stallabrass has suggested, "in the depiction of 'real life', there is no movement or development, only a still snapshot of the various forms of degradation. There is an odd comfort in this naturalism, as nostalgia is turned towards the present in the depiction of the enduring and unchanging British masses."[5] Currall's witty observations and fictional creations do precisely the opposite. They question the mediation of unquestioned beliefs, assuming a chameleon-like appearance. As witnesses to and participants in these works we are led to question the ground beneath our feet.

5 Stallabrass, p.280

Encyclopædia

Animal	Mineral	Vegetable	Phenomena

SOCIETY AND CULTURE

Society	History	People	Art and Leisure

SCIENCE AND INVENTION

Science	Engineering	Technology

ATLAS

The World	Europe

Animal	Mineral	Vegetable	Phenomena
Abalone	Animal	Arm	Bird
Blood	Body	Bone	Butterfly
Dinasaurs	Egg	Eye	Fish
Foot	Hair	Hand	Head
Human	Insect	Leech	Leg
Lion	Lizard	Magpie	Mammal
Man	Milk	Mollusc	Mouth
Muscle	Neck	Nits	Scale
Shell	Wing	Wren	

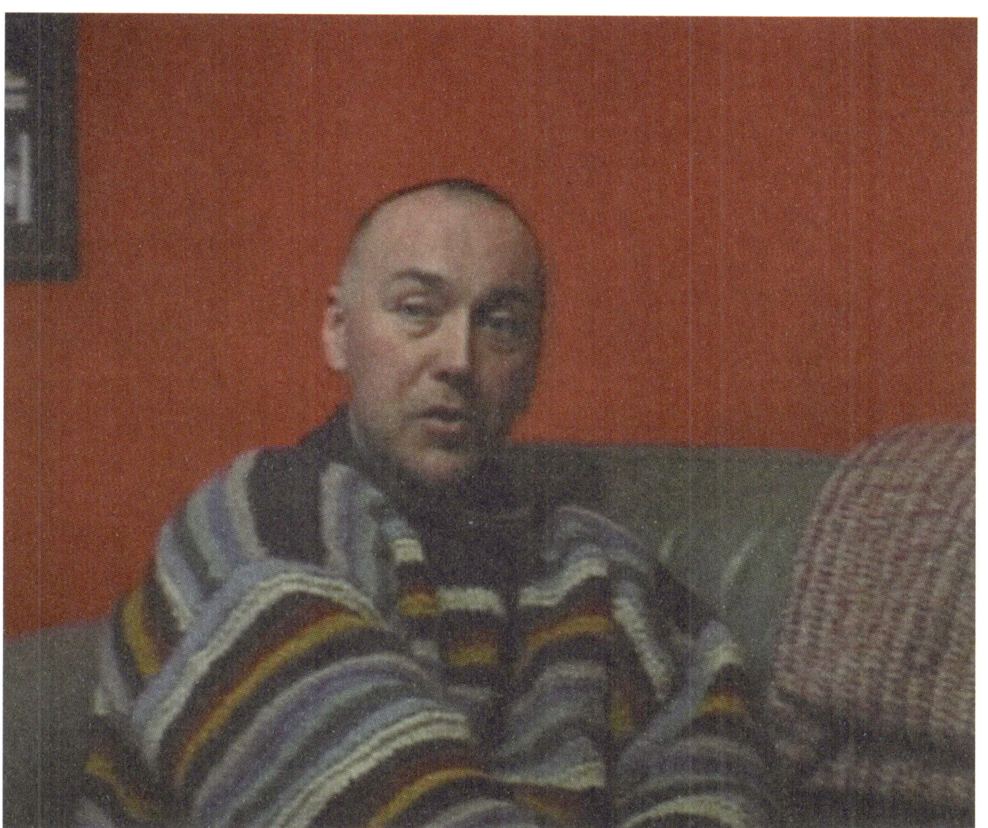

Blood is a pretty gory substance. Nobody likes blood.
Nobody likes to see blood,
but nobody likes to be without blood...
There is... You can give your blood to somebody else...
There is a shortage of blood...
Blood is... Blood is a red substance that flows through your body. It's warm.
You can be HOT blooded, which is a term that means you're quite aggressive...
You can be cold blooded, which means that you are very cold...
You can, or you can be an animal that's cold blooded, like a fish.

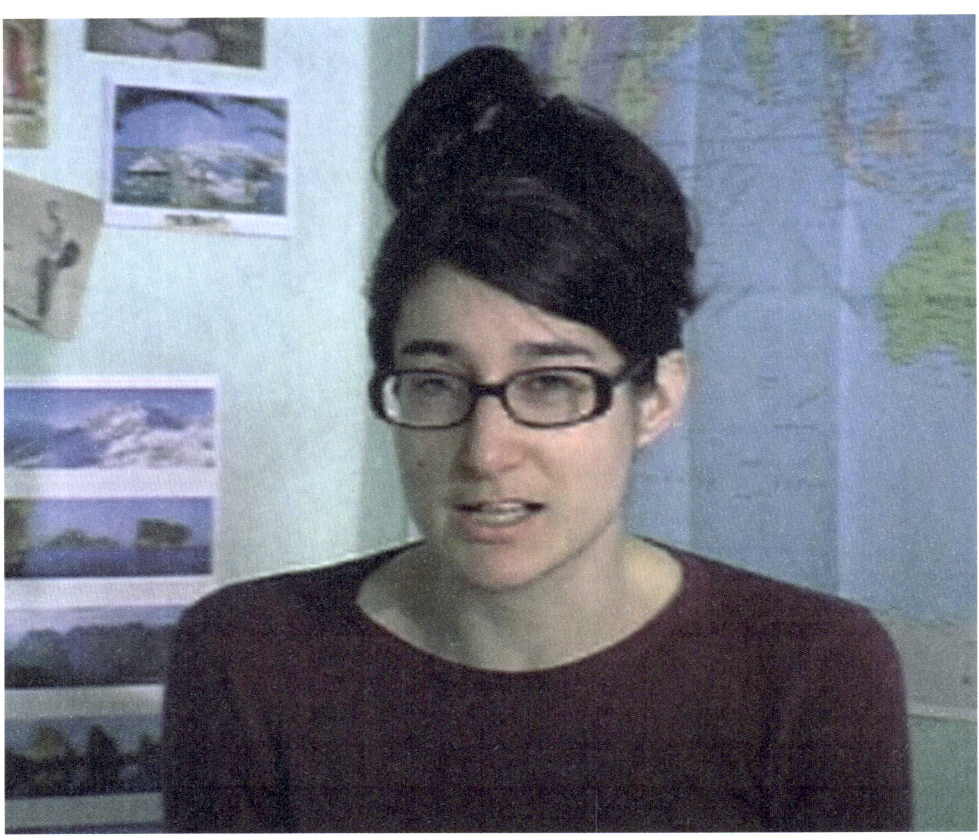

HOT

Hot is the opposite of cold.
It causes thermometers –
the mercury in thermometers –
to rise, er,
above zero,
quite a lot above zero...
Hot causes cold things such as ICE to melt, and chocolate to melt...
I think that's about it.

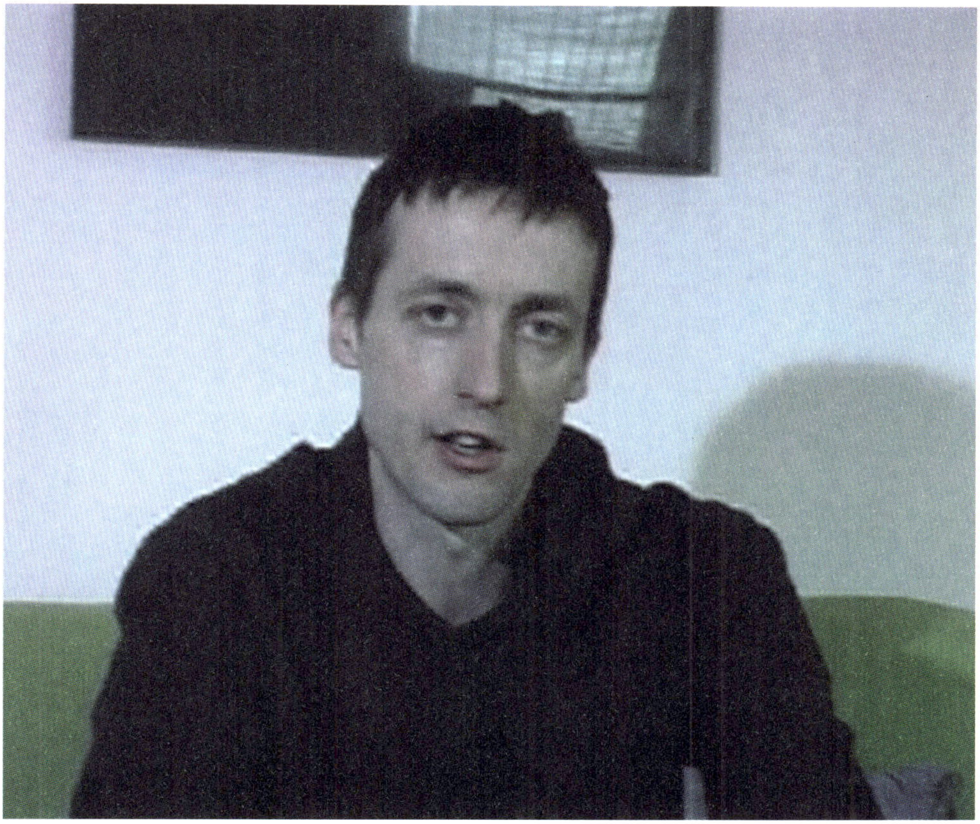

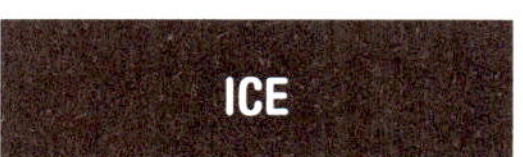

Ice.
Ice is basically frozen WATER. Very simply, erm, frozen WATER.
When WATER reaches nought degrees centigrade it turns into ice, which is a kind of firm, erm,
crystalline-like structure, very, very cold...
Things such as snow, hail, erm,
they're all forms of ice, erm,
y'know,
or even in your own fridge-freezer, you open that up, the what, the the kind of,
the glistening crystalline surface; that is ice as well.
So it's basically
frozen WATER.

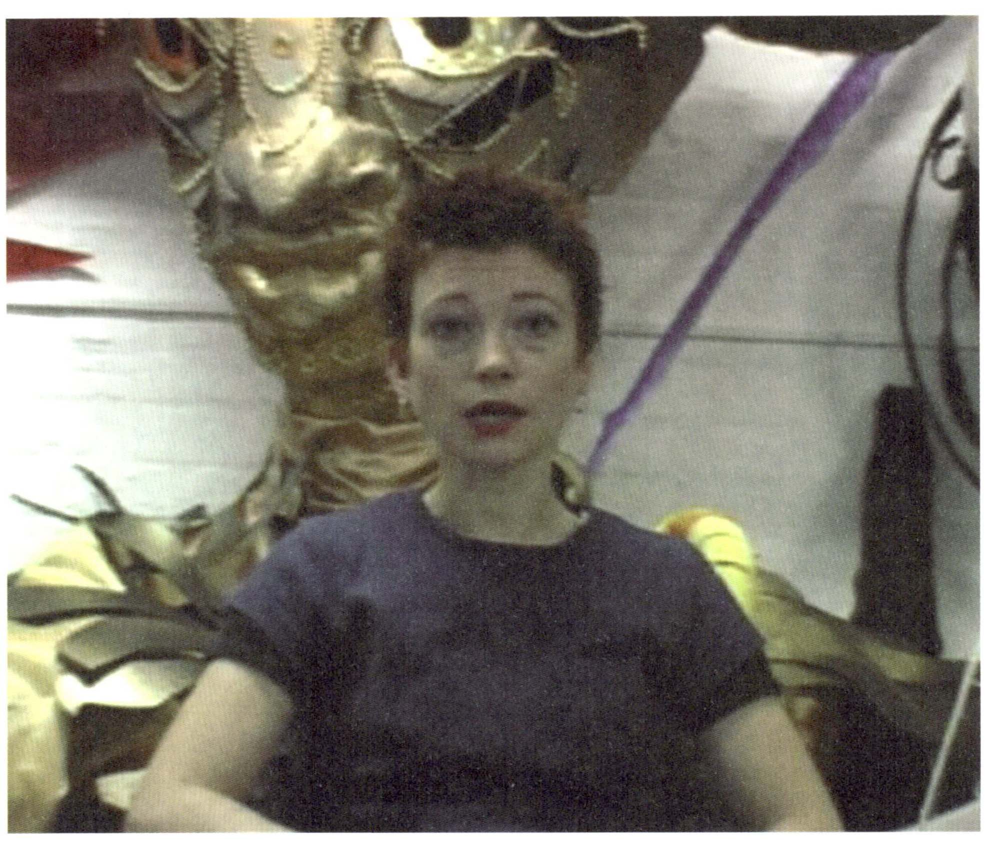

WATER

Water.
Water is, er, a liquid substance that is made up of, erm, hydrogen and OXYGEN (H_2O). Er...
Two parts hydrogen to one part OXYGEN. It, erm, falls from the sky as rain...
and also, when frozen, it becomes snow or ice...
You can put it... No, it comes from taps in this country. We get it out of a tap. But it's also what is the world is sort of comprised of, an awful lot of water; erm, in the seas, the rivers, erm, canals, all those kinds of things...
It's something that we should drink quite a lot of, but it has to be quite pure.
It shouldn't be like the stuff you get out of a canal... It's treated in this country and has a lot of fluoride and other substances put into it, for our benefit (supposedly), and also chlorine, to a certain extent, to keep it sort of clean...
You should drink seven pints of water a day. Our bodies are made up of an awful lot of water. [cough]
It keeps you healthy and fresh, if you're drinking it right, in the right amounts. You can put it...
You can make drinks with it, such as tea, and you can boil it up and it makes a refre...
tea and coffee and drinks like that...
It's in a lot of pop and you can buy it in bottles and it can be carbonated so it's fizzy.
Or you can have it still, like it comes out of our taps here...
You can put it in the freezer and make ice cubes for yourself (which is changing the consistency of it)...
People use water to wash themselves, erm, adding soap, and you can have baths in water and showers in water...
It's a really important part of what the world's made up of and what we're made up of,
and people take it for granted an awful lot.

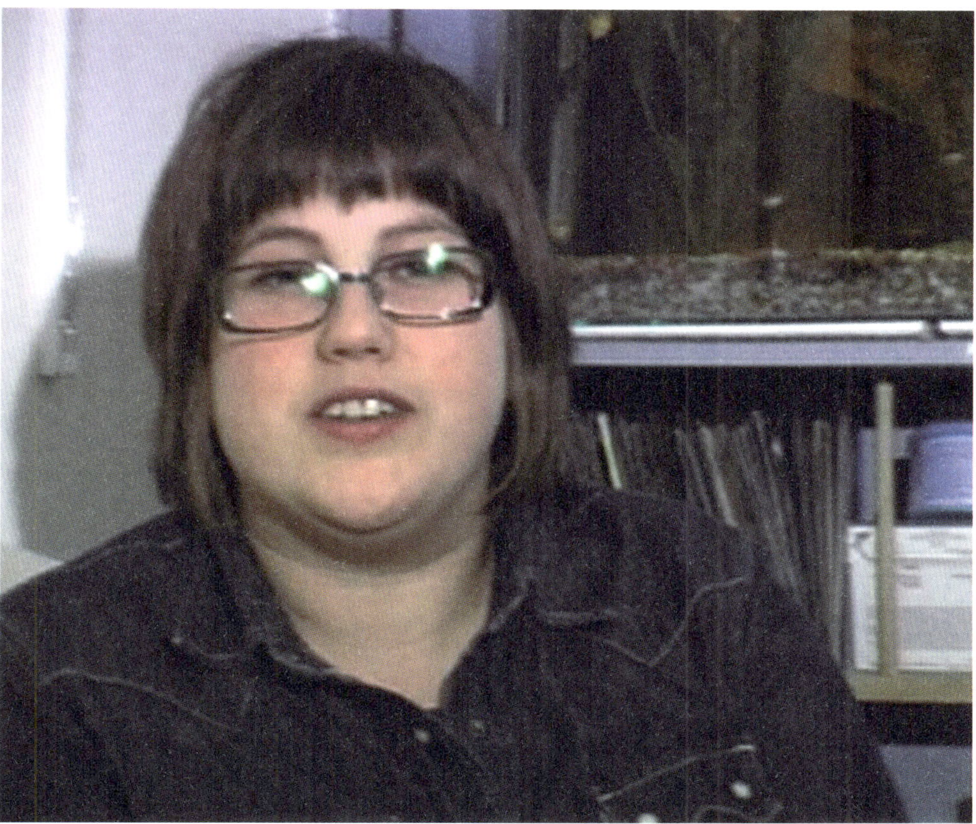

OXYGEN

Oxygen is an element...
It's on the periodic table under 'O', and it's one of the elements that makes up the world that we live in...
It's usually in the form of a gas...
which forms about twenty percent of the air that we breathe, but it's the part of the air that we breathe that, erm,
makes it possible for us to live. It's the, it's the gas that we use to, erm,
oxygenise our BLOOD, and therefore makes us live...
Oxygen, erm, can also form part of a corrosive action on certain materials, like metals, where oxygenisation
forms on the surface of the, of a metal, where the metal becomes in contact with air...
Rust is one of these oxidizations. Rust is an oxidization of iron.
Oxygen can be dissolved into some, erm, liquids...
Fish also use oxygen for part of their breathing, but their oxygen comes from the water that they live in...
Oxygen is part of the compound of water, so in a periodic table oxygen is 'O' and water is made up of oxygen
and Hydrogen and therefore water is H_2O,
because it has two hydrogens to one oxygen.

Encyclical on Encyclopædia – Sean Cubitt

It is traditional to start postmodern encyclopædic essays with a citation from Foucault, and specifically his citation of Jorge Luis Borges' citation of an imaginary Chinese encyclopædia whose categorisation of animals includes animals that from a long way off look like ants, fabulous, imaginary, included in the present classification, having just broken the water pot, and drawn with a fine camelhair brush. But I prefer an older and more piercing mind, the American modernist poet William Carlos Williams ('saxifrage is my flower/that splits the rocks'). In an extended experimental prose-poem composition, *The Descent of Winter*, written in 1927, published by Ezra Pound in *The Exile* in 1928, republished finally after half a century of obscurity in 1970 in an edition of Williams' early experiments by Webster Schott at New Directions. Williams was a doctor, a general practitioner in what was then industrial New Jersey. It is the end of the jazz age. The Wall Street Crash and the Great Depression are still two years in the future. Snatching writing time from his patients and his young family, Williams devotes himself to the double aesthetic attack that will guide him through his long poetic career, to capture the American voice, and to create a poetry of fact. But what is fact? And how is fact speakable? Here then is the passage I want to start from. What I like about it, and prefer in it over the glibness of Borges and the overworked citation from Foucault, is that the praxis of categorisation here is one that overwhelms the doctor. Where is the fact: in the symptom or the disease? How radical is experience? What is the meaning of the first word, the injunction which the writer places on the reader?

> Imagine a family of four grown men, one in bed with a sore throat, one with fresh
> plaster dust on his pants, one who played baseball all last summer and one holding the basin.

What are we to do with that command, to imagine the family? If you read on, there are other spartan scraps of description: the hot range, coats drying on chair backs. And then there is a paragraph transcribing the display ads from the Fairfield NJ newspaper. How are we to imagine that? As Gertrude Stein wrote, citing Laurence Sterne, would I had seen a polar bear, for how can I imagine one?

Categorial knowledge, the way we collate and structure data in the mind, is one of the most significant problems of contemporary psychology. It is also, of course, and for much the same reasons, a central issue in computer science, making it a central concern of linguistics too in that concatenation of mind, language and digital in the new paradigm of cognitive science. The question has an intriguing history. Francis Bacon, Lord Verulam, once falsely accused of writing the plays of Shakespeare by those who could not believe such oratory in the mouth of a commoner, first articulator of the scientific principles of observation and experiment, proposed a catalogue of all human knowledge founded on the three human faculties of memory, reason and imagination. Ramus, a century later, proposed a classificatory system of immense and startling complexity based on the matching of terms to create new zones of knowledge. But it was not until the 19th century, when libraries grew beyond the scale of human mnemonics, that the necessity of a durable classificatory schema for every branch of knowledge became pressing. Dewey, Library of Congress and Cutter systems, still ubiquitous in Western libraries, provided a systematic map. But they display oddities that betray their origins. LC, Library of Congress, for example, has ten major sections, of which one is agriculture, a suitable structure for a new and largely agricultural nation. Technology, however, is a sub-section, while other fields like mass media, computing, aerospace, bio-engineering and quantum physics unsurprisingly do not figure in the early versions, and had to have sub-sub-sections invented for them later.

LC's spectrum is now largely full. Like its 19th century cousins, LC aimed to provide a complete map; so every square on its grid was rapidly colonised, and each new entrant has to find an ever smaller sub-sub-sub-section on which to set up shop.

The problem was spotted in the early 1930s by Henry Evelyn Bliss, whose student Dr S.R. Ranganathan would, in a series of major innovations, present a new model for classification, the Colon system, widely used in new nations whose library services postdate the mid-20th century. Colon has a very different premise, classifying books not by their major topic alone, but by all the aspects under which it might be looked for. Tropical diseases of the liver in cattle, let's say, can fall obviously in four categories. The book's call number in Colon allows it to be found in all of them. It is, if you like, the grandfather of keyword searches. Indeed, Colon was subsequently a major inspiration for information retrieval design. As the international librarianship bodies march towards a semantic, machine-readable retrieval system, this model looks increasingly useful, not least because even at the end of his life, Ranganathan's system still only occupied about two-thirds of the alphabet. For all new fields of knowledge, the empty boxes lie waiting, along with the mechanisms for linking them to existing fields.

Bliss and Ranganathan's system gives the lie to one of the great theses on encyclopædic knowledge, the Whorff-Sapir hypothesis, according to which the categorial structure of a given natural language so structures the thinking of its speakers that they are unable to conceive of the world in terms other than those presented by the language. Thus, in one of Benjamin Lee Whorff's examples, a particular Native American language with only one tense does not allow its speakers to understand either history or planning, but contains their thought in an eternal present. Like MacLuhan's technological determinism, which argues that media technologies structure the mind of an epoch, the Whorff-Sapir hypothesis that language defines the thought of a people is never believed in public, but haunts the discourses of cultural critics. The central quandary is this: how could we think of something new, if language structures thought? How could language itself change, as it so obviously does?

The turn against Whorf and Sapir came first from the behaviourist psychologists, who simply ignored the unobservable inner mind and concentrated their attention on behaviours and their causes. In reaction to this constraining paradigm, Noam Chomsky proposed a novel form of linguistics. There is, he believes, a sort of language instinct in human beings, a mental structure that seeks out language and shapes it at its deepest level. As each baby comes into the world, it experiments with all the vocables in all the languages, but gradually narrows down on the ones proper to its home life: language, dialect. What the child acquires is, in Chomsky's terminology, competence. It internalises the rules for making sentences and the vocabulary of the tribe. It is able to understand and to make sentences which it has never heard before and which may never have been spoken or written before. That is competence.

Some cognitive scientists like to think of the process of sentence formation as a kind of dictionary exercise. The brain supplies a structure, let's say noun phrase/verb phrase, and then looks up the words to put into it in a sort of table. The look-up table model, however, is limited by the way it is imagined as a dictionary, that is, a book in which words are defined in terms of other words. Ted Nelson, father of hypertext, discovered the limitations of this system long ago in the 1970s when he began work on the extraordinary Project Xanadu. Part of the project involves teaching a computer common sense. Fed with snippets of ordinary knowledge (a house is smaller than a town, water flows downhill), the computer formulates questions to ascertain how they all fit together. For example, 'Is a man always older than his son?' and 'If I am in Washington, is my left foot in Washington also?' What Xanadu points up is that there is more than a dictionary involved in our use of language. There is a mental encyclopædia.

Last year Umberto Eco brought out a wonderfully challenging book called *Kant and the Platypus*. One of its central themes is the problem of categorial knowledge. In what form

do we know what we know about the world? What happens when something comes along
to disturb the forms of knowledge? Hence the platypus. It has a duck's bill, webbed feet and
lays eggs. It must be a bird. But it has warm blood, fur and suckles its young. It must be
a mammal. And of course it lives underwater and lays eggs like an amphibian. Aha. One
of Eco's points, which seems to bear out the Whorff-Sapir hypothesis, is the extraordinary
difficulty people had in seeing what was in front of them when confronted with this out-
landish challenge to right thinking. Even when a misfortunate specimen was dissected,
the best biological minds simply could not see the uterus. One thinks of the opposite case
too, when geographers added a vast inland sea occupying most of Alberta to their maps
because they had no other explanation for the rivers flowing away from the ocean along
the Canadian Rockies. The categorial mind plays endless tricks, not only in the dictionary,
but in the mind's encyclopædia.

—

Eco's emphasis is on the commonness of common sense. Common sense, the encyclopædia
shared by a tribe, is common because it is the fruit of dialogue. Among the entries some are
absolute – fire burns, never eat anything bigger than your head – and some are less so. Our
encyclopædias include entries on UFOs and dead Elvis sightings, on which we can discourse
at length, but in which for the most part we do not believe. But what they share is the
commonness of common sense. Most of us do not care whether a whale is a fish, but we
would correct a child who said so. And at the same time we can be persuaded of things we
hadn't believed before if enough people of the suitably trustworthy sort tell us that it is so.
Language, in short, is not fascist (as Roland Barthes had it) nor is it a virus from outer space
(as William S Burroughs believed for several hours in the 1960s). Language is profoundly
democratic. Chomsky's idea of competence is every schoolkid's ally: his idea is that our
competence is in the language we speak, not some ideal normative language like The Queen's
English. We should range these ideas of the encyclopædia against the formulaic and system-
atising projects to contain the whole of human knowledge in even the magically expanding
territory of Ranganathan's Colon classification. Knowledge is not administered: it grows.

—

It is such a shame that Foucault was French. After *Madame Bovary*, the great French
novelist Gustave Flaubert went on to start a never completed work called *Bouvard and
Pecuchet* whose eponymous heroes set out to acquire knowledge of all the great fields of
human endeavour, with invariably disastrous consequences. The first part of the book
details the idiocy of book-learning – the dictionary model. But the second drops even the
pretence of novel writing in the accepted sense and embarks instead on a staggeringly
inane dictionary of received thought. This is about where Foucault's thought begins. But
some few years into the twentieth century, the last novelist of them all (since the novel has
now either reverted to its origins as pulp fiction or more disastrously eked out a pretentious
afterlife in the annual award lists) reinvented the banality of the mental encyclopædia in an
altogether more warm-hearted, generous and democratic spirit. Here the two protagonists,
the 20th century Bouvard and Pecuchet, are walking back from a drunken night through
the dark streets of Dublin in 1904:

—

> Of what did the duumvirate deliberate during their itinerary?
> Music, literature, Ireland, Dublin, Paris, friendship, woman,
> prostitution, diet, the influence of gaslight or the light of arc
> and glow-lamps on the growth of adjoining paraheliotropic trees,
> exposed corporation emergency dustbuckets, the Roman catholic
> church, ecclesiastical celibacy, the Irish nation, jesuit education,
> careers, the study of medicine, the past day, the maleficent influence
> of the presabbath, Stephen's collapse...

—

The alert reader will know who is speaking on each of these topics, who is likely to say
what. You would also be taken on the one hand with the banality of the conversation, its
proximity to Flaubert's dictionary (Latin women: hot-blooded, carry knives; English women:
good legs, good complexions from all the rain, cold fish). But on the other, you should also

be awake to the great cast of their thoughts and their dialogue, to the fact that among all
the banalities they are speaking of art, of science, of religion, of history, of the destiny of
their country and of each other. Joyce's Bloom and Dedalus are not buffoons, or not only
buffoons, but also the heroic navigators of a modern Odyssey at last on the final approach
to Ithaca and home. For Foucault, the encyclopædia is delivered from on high, a papal bull
impressed upon mindless devotees. For Joyce, it is a constant work of construction through
mutual dialogue, trust and generosity. Do you think, we might still be asking, half-cut after
some Saturday night binge and missing the last bus home, those trees grow towards the
streetlights? And from those deliberations a new mode of knowledge opening like a flower.

It shouldn't need repeating that the computer is neither a story-telling nor a depicting
machine at heart. Too many of our commentators on digital media as a space for art believe
that the computer in some way derives from the novel and the cinema, and spend their time
telling us how computers differ from those older leisure and entertainment forms. But the
computer began life as a calculator, and expanded on the back of its use in the manipulation
of statistics, the storage and retrieval of data, and the visual or graphic presentation of graphs
and maps, not pictures. At the heart of the computer revolution lie accountancy programmes
(spreadsheets) and filing programmes (databases): these applications are the reasons we have
computers on our desks. That is why Currall's intervention in the expert system of digital
databasing is so much more advanced than the parallel attempts to break up narrative or
to disrupt realist depictions, as though at the beginning of the 21st century we needed
to repeat the work of the beginning of the 20th. While we wait impatiently for the first
artist of the spreadsheet, we have here a work that goes straight for the structure and the
definitional nature of the database, a work engaging with central issues in computer culture.

Currall's encyclopædia is of the Ecoesque variety. It is full of ordinary wisdom, from
the life of the wren and how to recognise it to the arbitrariness of temporal measurement.
Like all true encyclopædia, it is not exclusively verbal, but is ripe with hand gestures that
shape and describe phenomena. Certainties melt under the scrutiny of their formalisation.
Well, what is time? In dictionary terms, not so difficult: the measurement of change. But in
encyclopædic terms, the problem is more complex, demanding exemplification. And examples
breed complexity and uncertainty. Most of all, they beg our intervention, beg us to join in
the chase of complex abstract notions or indeed of common objects. Can we add to and refine
the description of insects? Of course: the mode of common sense is such that it is never
complete, and the pursuit of wisdom and knowledge is not bounded by the scientific criteria
of truth as provable and demonstrable, but by the other scientific principle of falsifiability.
Every natural encyclopædia – natural by analogy with the natural languages, those that
have evolved in societies as opposed to artificial languages like Esperanto and mathematics
– every natural encyclopædia is an open system, evolving through and towards a never
complete, never totalised knowledge. At the same time, it is a collective resource of practical
skills, of how to's and when to's.

You begin to notice how often people intersperse their descriptions (encyclopædias are
descriptive, not definitive) with invitations to experiment, to try out, to make or do something as a way of ensuring the knowledge. These are not the bare facts of the world: they
are the processes in which we approximate our language, our culture and our actions in
the world with the world's own rules and actions. Currall is wise. The dictionary and the
definitive encyclopædias of the library catalogues are indeed, as Foucault accuses them,
fascist in their attempt at total control of knowledge and even of possible knowledge. But
in this world of common, descriptive and evolving sense-making, Currall's encyclopædia
is democratic and, even more so, evolutionary. The interactions occur as imitations of the
links we make in our own mental encyclopædias, but they are something more. They indicate
the participation of the machine in the ordering of common sense today. To the extent that
this participation is an involvement in human knowledge of another species, surely we can
see in *Encyclopædia* the beginnings of an art in which democracy extends towards the non-
human: an ecological aesthetic.

and other works

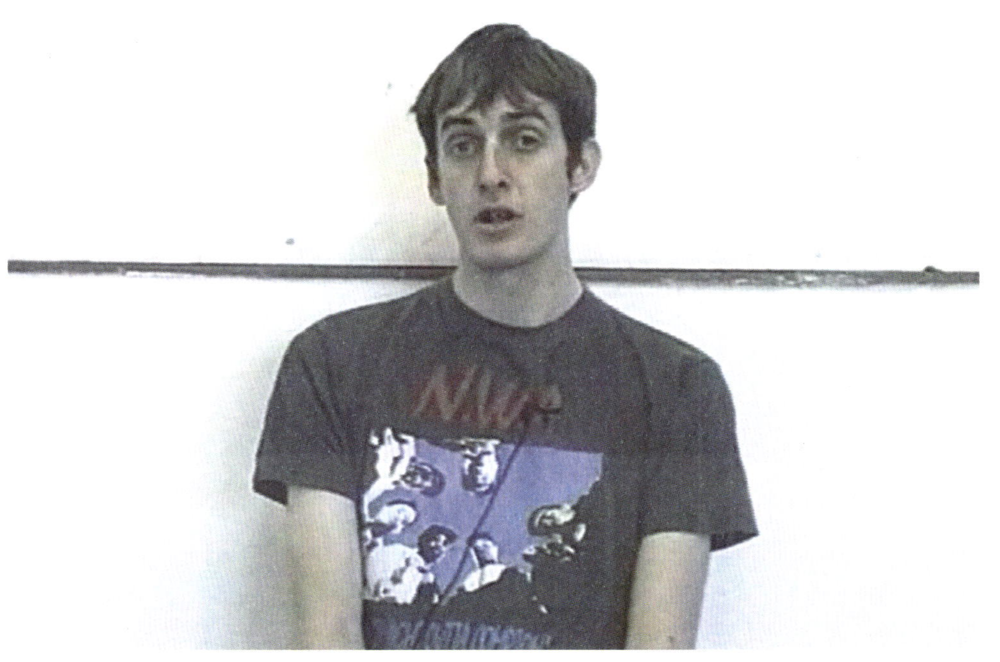

Well, erm... We were flying over central Scotland, and we got buzzed by a couple of airforce jets and we had to make a crash landing. Erm... We came down, er, just east of Stirling... no j'- no, just west of Stirling. We had to abandon the ship because we thought it was going to blow, for a while, and we hid it, we've got it under a cloaking device now and well... we made our way to, well I came to Glasgow. There was five of us on board. We've all got various jobs and things now. Well actually, no, one of us is on the dole. Erm... I decided, erm, to be an artist because I'd always been good at drawing, and... er... I got a, I got a job one day a week at the art school and that's good because, erm, I get to meet a lot of people from all over, it's quite cosmopolitan. Erm, it's interesting, er, we had to erm... Fortunately, we go polymorphous and we can change our shape to whatever we want to. We thought it best to go human because there seemed to be more of them, and, er, they're least likely to notice us. Erm... I - I decided to be English because I wasn't very good at the Scottish accent. Erm... Looking forward to getting back home. Erm... Two of the crew are now working at a vehicle repair shop and, er, they're picking up bits and pieces with which we eventually hope to get the ship back and running again, er, maybe by the end of the year. I'll miss it here, yeah, I shall miss it, er... Er, had quite a bit of success with the art lately and, er, it's nothing that would really go down well back on my planet, so, er, I'll have to abandon all that and I'm quite enjoying it. But of course, I miss home and it's – it's quite a good job I've got anyway, like, flying flying-saucers er... perph! That's about it really...............................Okay?

Jetsam – 1995

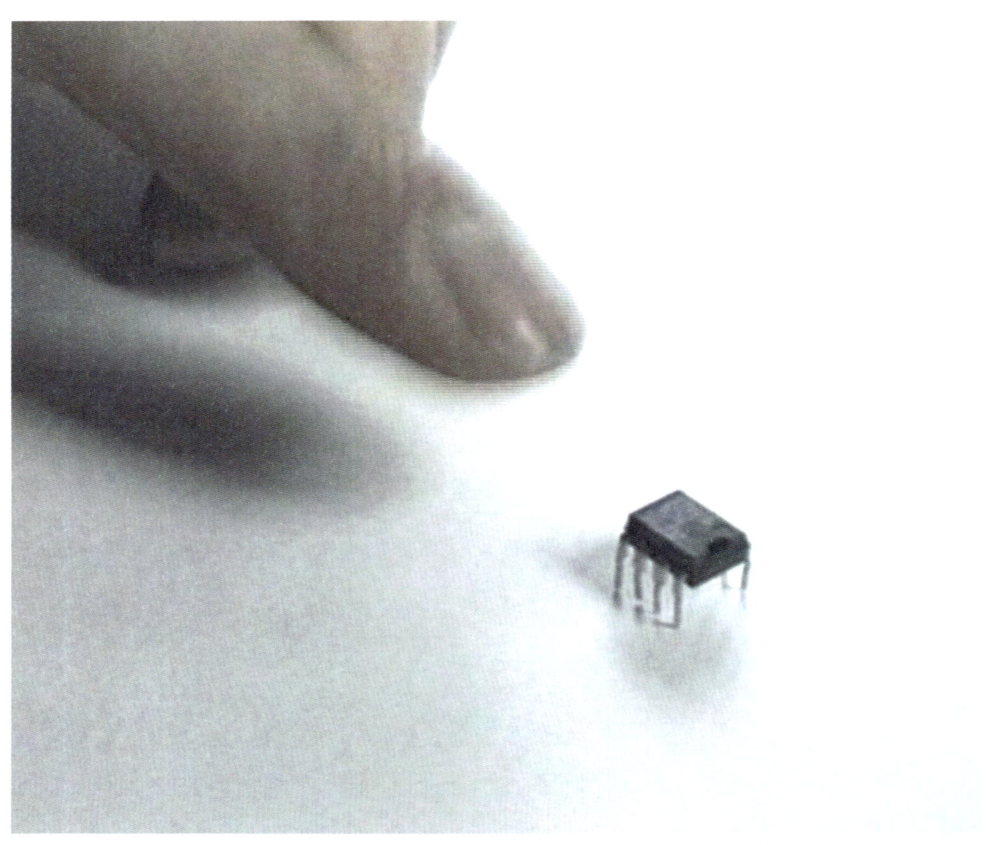

Right then. Now, what I want you to do is: every time I press down on the keyboard, on one of the letters on the keyboard, I want you to put that letter up on the screen in front of me. OK? Now, every time I press down on one of the numbers on the keyboard I want you to do the same with that. I want you to put it up on the screen in front of me.

Word Processing – 1995

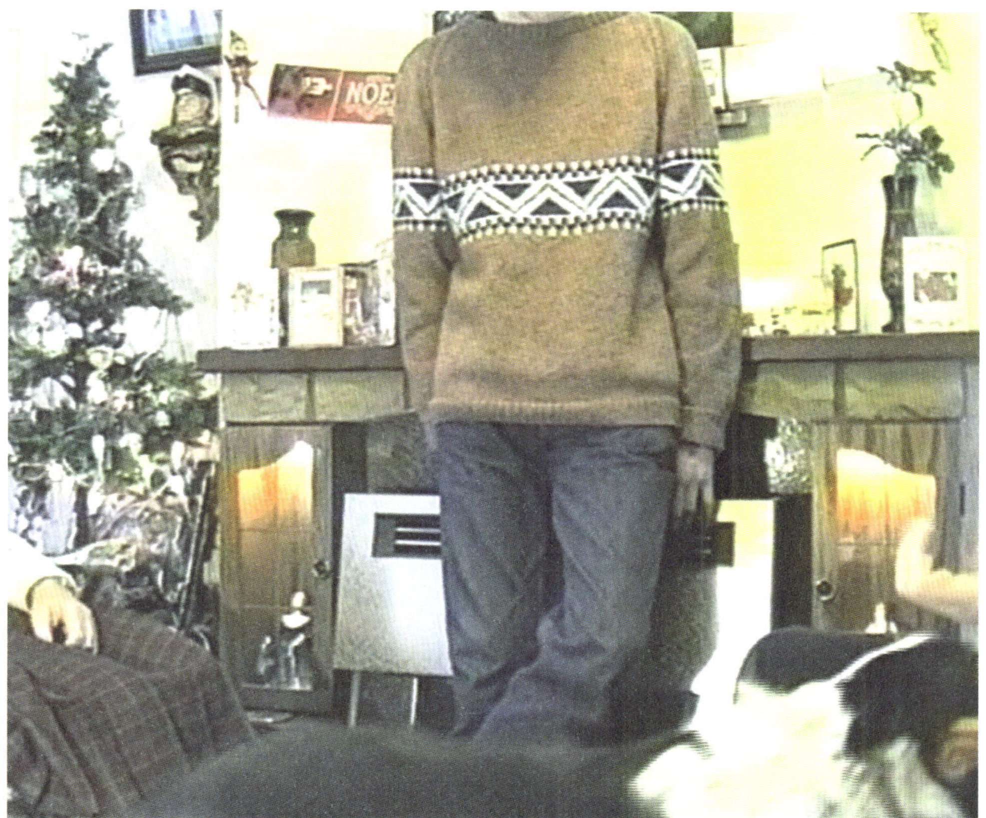

Where will I sleep?
If you've got a board what you'll probably as well have to try and think of to take is probably a piece of rope which you could tie yourself to the board. Because if you slept and you rolled off you would drown. The chances of getting back on that would be very remote because of the floating – so you would have to take something and be prepared to tie yourself on to it.

How will I keep warm and dry?
This extra clothing you've got with you will have to keep you dry as well. You could probably try and take with you a very light weight plastic mac which you could wear over the top of everything so that, that what you'd got on would be dry. If it did get wet, during the day you could perhaps dry it out by actually, if you like, holding it up or anything. Try and find some method of drying your stuff out so that you're keeping yourself rather dry.

This is taking it for granted you're on a raft though. If you're just in the water there's no way you can keep dry. Just in the water it's just a matter of keeping afloat as long as you can, making as much noise as you can, to attract attention. Other than that, there's nothing.

Survival Kits: Shipwreck, Plane Crash, Nuclear War – 1996

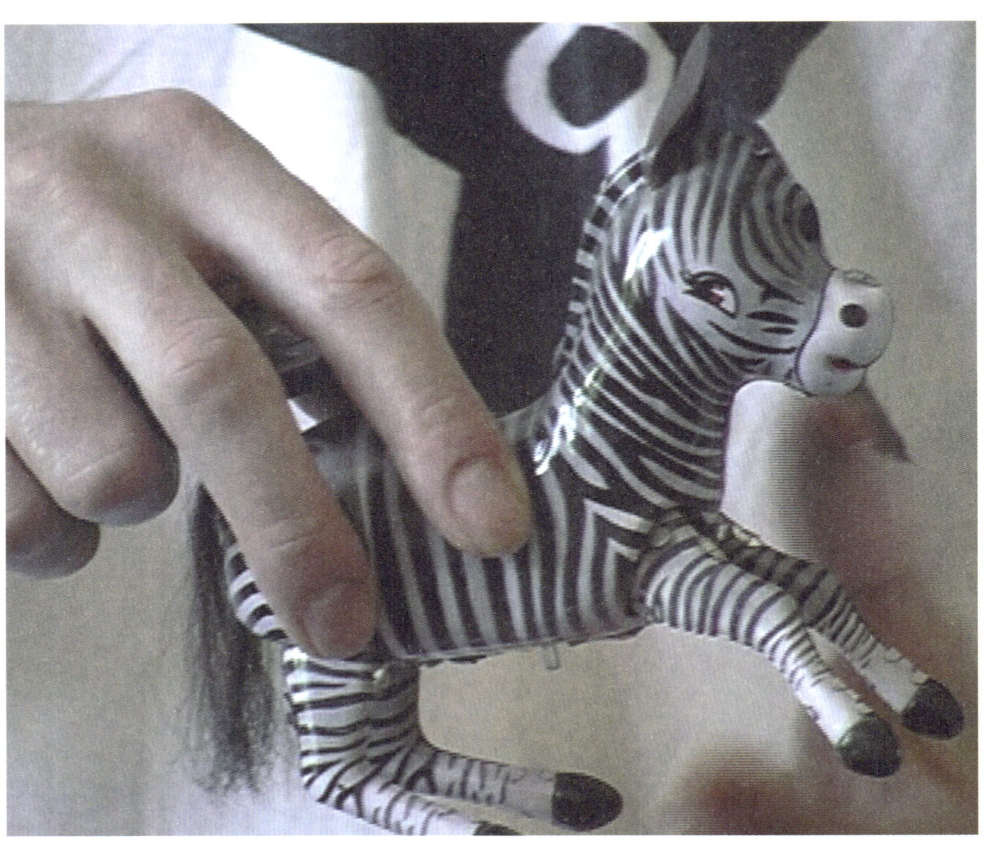

This was a toy belonging to my great grand mother ...look at the dust on that... It's so old in fact that it's made out of tin. It was passed down to me when I was just a child. It's wind-up. It's got a clockwork mechanism down here. I've lost the key for it long since, and It doesn't actually work very well anymore anyway. But, as you can see it's tin, very old, and it is a collectable item as well, because it's so old and because it's tin and because it's a family heirloom. It's a jumping zebra. When you wind it up it goes like that, and jumps. Very beautiful, very old and of course I'd never want to part with this. I'd better put it back in its box before it gets broken.

From the eighteen nineties I think.

Lying About Myself In Order To Appear More Interesting – 1999

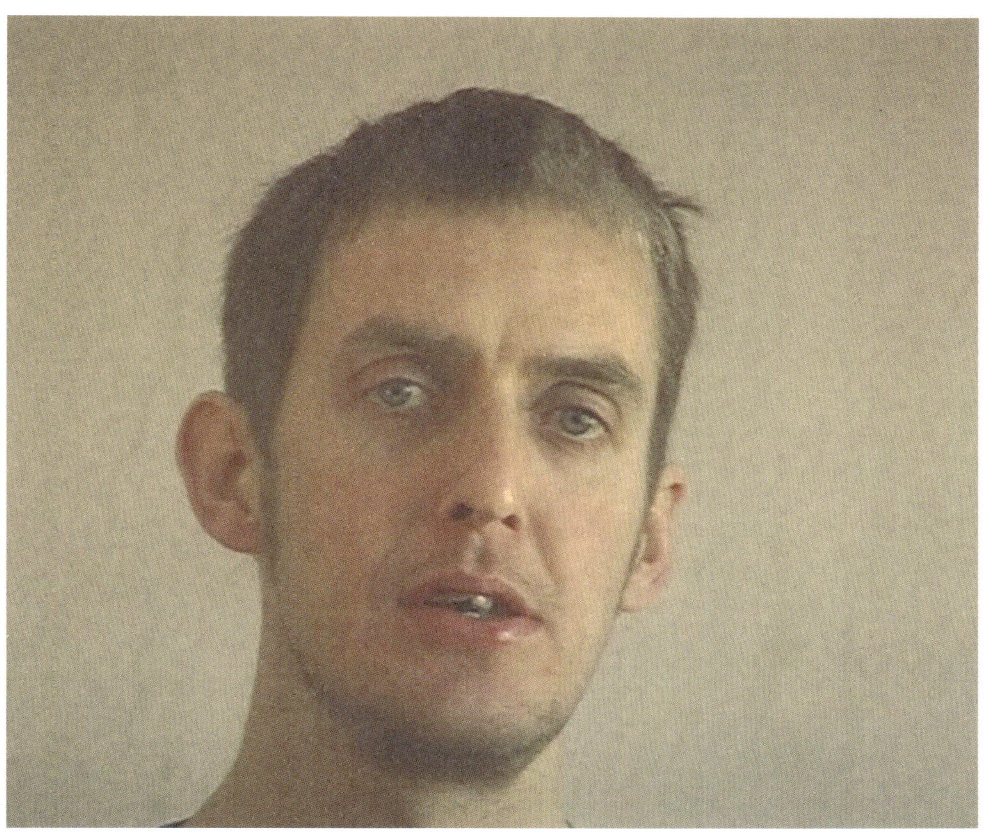

Message To My Best Friend – 2000

Acknowledgements

Encyclopædia and other works
Potteries Museum and Art Gallery Stoke-on-Trent 13 May - 2 July 2000
Stills Edinburgh 8 August - 23 September 2000

Exhibition curated and produced by Film and Video Umbrella,
Potteries Museum and Art Gallery and Stills

Encyclopædia CD ROM supported by the
New Media Projects fund of the Arts Council of England
Encyclopaedia was made possible with support of the
1998 Richard Hough Bursary

Encyclopædia and other works
Published by Film and Video Umbrella
© 2000, Film and Video Umbrella
Publication supported by a Regional Arts Lottery Programme award
from West Midlands Arts

Designed by Richard Bonner-Morgan
Printed by Geoff Neal Litho

Thanks to: Mike Jones, Caroline Smith and Keith Whittle at Film and Video Umbrella;
Andrea Davidson at the Arts Council of England; Mark Dey at West Midlands Arts.

Film and Video Umbrella
Rugby Chambers 2 Rugby Street London WC1N 3QZ
T 020 7831 7753 F 020 7831 7746
E info@fvu.co.uk W www.fvumbrella.com

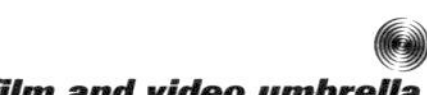
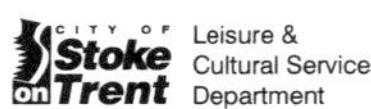

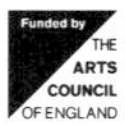
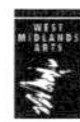